Stories from Faiths

SIKHISM

Sujatha Menon

Heinemann

www.heinemannlibrary.co.uk
Visit our website to find out more information about Heinemann Library books.

To order:
☎ Phone +44 (0) 1865 888066
🖹 Fax +44 (0) 1865 314091
💻 Visit www.heinemannlibrary.co.uk

Heinemann Library is an imprint of Capstone Global Library Limited, a company incorporated in England and Wales having its registered office at 7 Pilgrim Street, London, EC4V 6LB – Registered company number: 6695582

"Heinemann" is a registered trademark of Pearson Education Limited, under licence to Capstone Global Library Limited

Editor: Honor Head
Designer: Harleen Mehta
Picture Researchers: Nikhil Verma
Art Director: Rahul Dhiman
Client Service Manager: Aparna Malhotra
Project Managers: Smita Mehta, Santosh Vasudevan
Lineart: Sibi N Devasia
Colouring Artists: Subhash Vohra, Danish Zaidi, Ashish Tanwar
Originated by Chroma Graphics (Overseas) Pte Ltd
Printed and bound in China by CTPS

ISBN 978-0-431-08225-7 (hardback)
13 12 11 10 09
10 9 8 7 6 5 4 3 2 1

ISBN 978-0-431-08232-5 (paperback)
14 13 12 11 10
10 9 8 7 6 5 4 3 2 1

British Library Cataloguing in Publication Data
Menon, Sujatha, 1975–
    Sikhism. – (Stories from faiths)
    294.6
A full catalogue record for this book is available from the British Library.

Acknowledgements

We would like to thank the following for permission to reproduce photographs (t = top, b = bottom, c = centre, l = l eft, r = right, m = middle): Ajmone Tristano/ Shutterstock: 4mr, Holger Mette/ Shutterstock: 5, Shiv Kumar Pushpakar/ The Hindu: 7tr, Munish Byala/ Reuters: 9tr, Davinder Luther/ Associated Press: 11tr, K R Deepak/ The Hindu: 12tl, Anjum Naveed/ Associated Press: 15tr, Anjum Naveed/ Associated Press: 16tl, Luciano Mortula/ Shutterstock: 19tr, Aman Sharma/ Associated Press: 20tl, Aman Sharma/ Associated Press: 23tr, Salamanderman/ Shutterstock: 24bl, Mandeep Singh: 27tr, Takhat Sachkhand Sri Hazur sahib: 28tl

Q2A Media Art Bank: 6, 8, 10–11, 12–13, 14–15, 16–17, 18, 20–21, 22, 24–25, 26–27, 29.

Cover photograph of a young Sikh at a prayer vigil reproduced with permission of Marco Secchi/ Alamy.

We would like to thank Q2AMEDIA for invaluable help in the preparation of this book.

Every effort has been made to contact copyright holders of material reproduced in this book. Any omissions will be rectified in subsequent printings if notice is given to the publishers.

Disclaimer

All the Internet addresses (URLs) given in this book were valid at the time of going to press. However, due to the dynamic nature of the Internet, some addresses may have changed, or sites may have changed or ceased to exist since publication. While the author and publishers regret any inconvenience this may cause readers, no responsibility for any such changes can be accepted by either the author or the publishers.

Contents

Some words are printed in bold, **like this**. You can find out what they mean in the glossary.

What is Sikhism?

Sikhism is the fifth largest religion in the world. It was founded about 500 years ago in the Punjab region of India and Pakistan by Guru Nanak, the first Sikh Guru. In those days **Hindus** and **Muslims** were often at war. Guru Nanak tried to bring the two groups together by preaching that there was only one God. This formed the foundation for Sikhism. Today, Sikhs live in many different countries around the world. Large groups of Sikhs live in big cities such as London, Toronto and Los Angeles.

Beliefs

Sikhs believe in one God who has no form or name. They call God by many names. The most common is *Waheguru*, which means "the wonderful Lord" in **Punjabi**. A Sikh place of worship is called a **gurdwara**. Most of the Sikh ceremonies, such as **baptisms** and marriages, take place in the gurdwara. Hamandir Sahib in Amritsar, India, also known as the Golden Temple, is the most popular of all gurdwaras.

The Ten Gurus

The word *Guru* means "teacher" in Sanskrit, an ancient Indian language. Sikhs follow the teachings of the **Ten Gurus**, which have been recorded in their holy book – the **Guru Granth Sahib**. Guru Nanak was the first Guru while Guru Gobind Singh was the tenth Guru. Most stories from Sikhism are based on the lives of the Gurus.

The Golden Temple in Amritsar is covered in real gold and is one of the most beautiful gurdwaras in the world.

A Message from God

A long time ago, there was a boy named Nanak who lived in a village near Lahore, Pakistan. Nanak was not like the other boys of his age. While the other boys played, Nanak spent his time praying and helping the poor. As he grew older, Nanak became more religious. He didn't want to be rich, and gave most of the money he earned to the poor.

Nanak's day always began with a dip in the river nearby. One day, he plunged into the river and never came out. His friends and family looked everywhere for him.

Guru Nanak liked to go for a swim in a river close to his home every morning.

They finally gave up, thinking he had drowned.

Nanak didn't drown, but simply disappeared into another world where he met God. While everyone was out looking for him, God was telling Nanak to spread His message of peace among the people.

Three days after he vanished, Nanak reappeared on the riverbank. The villagers were shocked.

"Where did you go? We were worried!" they said. Nanak didn't utter a word. A few days later when he finally broke his silence, Nanak said, "There is no **Hindu**, no **Muslim**. There is but one God." He then told the villagers all that he had learned from God in those three days.

Word soon spread about a saint who had met God, and people began to flock to see Nanak. They started calling him Guru. This is how Guru Nanak founded Sikhism and became its first Guru.

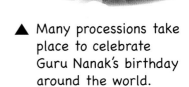

▲ Many processions take place to celebrate Guru Nanak's birthday around the world.

Guru Nanak Gurpurab

Guru Nanak **Dev**'s birthday, known as Guru Nanak Gurpurab, is one of the most important Sikh festivals. It is celebrated around the world. The celebrations last for three days. During this time the **Guru Granth Sahib** is read continuously for two days in **gurdwaras**. On the third day, hymns are sung in praise of Guru Nanak followed by **langar**, a **communal** lunch.

Guru Nanak and the Saints of Multan

Guru Nanak travelled far and wide to spread God's message. His trusted **disciple**, Mardana, accompanied him everywhere. One day, Guru Nanak arrived in the Punjab town of Multan, which is now in Pakistan. The **pirs**, or holy men, of Multan had heard a great deal about the Guru and they felt threatened.

Guru Nanak placed a flower in the cup and asked Mardana to return it to the holy men of Multan.

"What do we do? How do we ask Nanak to leave without hurting his feelings?" the pirs wondered. Finally, they came up with a plan. They sent Guru Nanak a cup filled to the brim with milk.

Guru Nanak placed a flower on top and sent it back to the pirs.

"**Guruji**, is it not rude to return a present?" Mardana asked.

Guru Nanak smiled, "Mardana, there lies a hidden message within this present. The pirs wanted to tell me that just like the cup filled to the brim, Multan is already full of saints, and that there is no room for another one. My answer is that as there is room for the flower in the cup of milk, there is always room for more religious teachers in this world."

When the pirs received Guru Nanak's message, they felt ashamed of what they had done. They visited the Guru and asked his forgiveness.

▲ Sikhs on their way to celebrate the festival of **Baisakhi** at Nankana Sahib. On their heads they carry the **Guru Granth Sahib**, the holy book of Sikhism.

Nankana Sahib

The small town where Guru Nanak was born is now called Nankana Sahib. It is one of the most sacred places of the Sikhs. The town is located near Lahore in Pakistan. Thousands of Sikh pilgrims from India cross the border between India and Pakistan every year to visit Nankana Sahib. The town has nine gurdwaras. **Gurdwara** Janam Asthan is built on the site where Guru Nanak was believed to have been born.

The Honest Carpenter

In the village of Saidpur in Pakistan, there lived a hard-working carpenter called Bhai Lalo. He was honest and kind. One day, Bhai Lalo was at his workshop, when he saw two holy men walking towards him. The holy men were Guru Nanak and Mardana.

As the men approached his house, Bhai Lalo set aside his work, "Welcome to my home. You must be tired and thirsty. Please be seated while I get some water."

While the two men rested, Bhai Lalo went into the kitchen and asked his wife to make lunch.

Bhai Lalo served a simple meal of bread and lentils. "Hmmm. The food is so simple yet very delicious," said Mardana, clearly enjoying his meal.

"That is because Bhai Lalo earned this food through honesty and hard work," Guru Nanak replied.

After the meal, Bhai Lalo requested the Guru to stay with him for a few days. Guru Nanak accepted his kind invitation.

▲ Sometimes hundreds of people turn up for the langar.

Bhai Lalo served the holy men bread and lentils.

Langar

Guru Nanak believed that all humans were equal in the eyes of God. He therefore started the custom of **langar**. This is a meal in which people of all religions and colour, rich and poor eat together in one place. Langar is served twice a day throughout the year in **gurdwaras**.

▲ Sikhs always cover their heads as a sign of respect before entering a gurdwara.

Gurdwara

A Sikh place of worship is called a gurdwara. The word *gurdwara* means "doorway to the Guru" in the **Punjabi** language. People from all religions are allowed to enter the gurdwara. Guru Nanak believed that God did not have any form and so gurdwaras do not have statues or paintings of God.

Meanwhile, a rich man named Malik Bhago heard that Guru Nanak had arrived at Saidpur. He was upset that such a well-known holy man was staying with a poor carpenter.

Malik Bhago arranged a huge feast in Guru Nanak's honour and invited him to stay with him. But Guru Nanak turned down the invitation.

Malik Bhago was furious. "Why do you prefer a carpenter's dry bread to the delicious feast I offer?" he asked.

Guru Nanak sent for Malik Bhago's feast and Bhai Lalo's simple meal. He took the dry bread from Bhai Lalo in one hand and Malik Bhago's sweet pancake in the other and squeezed them.

Everyone present gasped as milk dripped from Bhai Lalo's dry bread and blood oozed out of Malik Bhago's pancake!

"Bhai Lalo's bread was earned through hard work and honesty, while Malik Bhago, you cheated people to become rich. Why would I prefer your food to Bhai Lalo's meal that is as pure as milk?" Guru Nanak explained.

"You are right," Malik Bhago said, hanging his head in shame, "please forgive me. In future I shall make sure I treat people with honesty and kindness."

Bhai Lalo and Malik Bhago looked shocked as milk flowed from Bhai Lalo's bread and blood dripped from Malik Bhago's pancake!

13

The Story at Panja Sahib

Once, while travelling, Guru Nanak stopped to rest at the foot of a hill in a small town, in Pakistan. As the news of the Guru's arrival spread through the town, people flocked to meet him.

Mardana begged Kandhari to release the water from the spring, but Kandhari refused to do so.

A saint named Baba Wali Kandhari watched the Guru and his followers from his house on top of the hill. When he saw how popular the Guru was, Kandhari grew jealous of him.

"No one comes to visit me anymore. How can I drive this new saint away?" Kandhari thought as he paced up and down. Suddenly, an idea struck him. The spring that flowed near his house was the only source of water for the village below. He hoped that if he blocked the water supply, people would get angry and ask the Guru to leave. So he hauled a few boulders over to the stream and blocked the water.

When the villagers realised what had happened, they asked Kandhari to help them.

"Why don't you ask your great Guru to help you? If he is as powerful as everyone says he is, he should be able to produce water even from a rock," Kandhari said.

▲ There are no idols inside a **gurdwara**. Sikhs bow before their holy book, the Guru Granth Sahib.

The Holy Book

The **Guru Granth Sahib** is the holy book of the Sikhs. It contains the teachings of Guru Nanak and the nine gurus who followed him. The first volume, Adi Granth, was compiled by Guru Arjan **Dev**, the fifth guru. The holy book consists of 1,430 pages of **shabads** (hymns) of the **Ten Gurus**.

▲ Thousands of Sikhs visit the famous rock at the Panja Sahib every year.

The Panja Sahib

Gurdwara Panja Sahib, in the town of Hasan Abdal in Northern Punjab, contains the rock Guru Nanak stopped. It has his hand print on it. Every year thousands of Sikhs visit Panja Sahib during the harvest festival to see the hand print and pray to Guru Nanak.

The villagers rushed to the Guru with their problem.

Guru Nanak turned to his **disciple**, saying, "Mardana, why don't you try talking to Kandhari?" So Mardana climbed up the hill to reason with the jealous saint, but Kandhari wouldn't listen.

The villagers grew desperate. "What do we do, **Guruji**?" they asked.

Guru Nanak pointed to a huge rock nearby. "Move that rock aside."

The villagers did as they were told and fresh water gushed out of the ground where the rock stood. The villagers gasped with amazement and danced about happily.

Kandhari, who was watching from the hilltop, grew so angry that he pushed a boulder down the hill towards Guru Nanak.

When the people saw the huge rock rolling down, they shrieked, "Guruji, look out!"

Guru Nanak smiled and raised his right hand to stop the boulder in its tracks. When Kandhari saw this, he rushed down the hill and fell at the Guru's feet. "Oh, Great One, please forgive me my sins," he pleaded.

Guru Nanak smiled and hugged Kandhari, who from then on became one of his followers.

Guru Nanak stopped the huge rock with his hand.

The Pot of Honey

Kattu Shah was a keen follower of Guru Har Gobind, the sixth Guru. He led a humble life in a small village in Kashmir.

Kattu Shah returned the pot of honey to his guests and waved goodbye as they went on their way to visit the Guru.

Kattu Shah was very devoted and prayed to God all the time, just as his Guru had told him to. He even forgot to eat and sleep. Soon Kattu grew thin and tired, but that didn't stop him from thinking about God.

One day, a group of Guru Har Gobind's followers arrived at Kattu's doorstep. "We are on our way to meet **Guruji**. Can we please rest here for a while?" they asked.

Kattu went out of his way to make the pilgrims comfortable. Just as they were leaving, Kattu noticed one of them carrying a pot of honey. "May I see what's in the pot?" he asked softly.

The guests opened the pot. "May I taste the honey?" Kattu asked peeking into the pot.

"Kattu, this is an offering for Guruji. We can't let you taste it as it will become impure," the pilgrims replied.

"You're right," agreed Kattu and waved goodbye as his guests went on their way.

▲ The Golden Temple is also known as Harmandir Sahib.

The Golden Temple

The Golden Temple is one of the most important **gurdwaras** in the world. It is located in the city of Amritsar in Punjab, India. It was built by Guru Arjan **Dev**, the fifth Guru of the Sikhs. The gurdwara was originally not made of gold. Much of the gold and marble decoration was done during the time of Maharaja Ranjit Singh, Emperor of Punjab.

Sikhs light lamps on Diwali to celebrate the release of Guru Har Gobind and the princes.

Diwali

In 1619, Guru Har Gobind, the sixth Guru, and 52 Indian princes were imprisoned by Jehangir, the **Mughal** ruler. When Jehangir offered to free him, Guru Har Gobind demanded that the 52 princes also be freed. Jehangir agreed to release all those who could hold on to the Guru's cloak. Guru Har Gobind had a cloak with 52 strings made so that all of them could walk out of the prison holding on to the strings. When the Guru arrived at the Golden Temple in Amritsar, his followers lit lamps to celebrate.

When the pilgrims reached Guru Har Gobind's camp, they offered him the pot of honey. "Guruji, please accept our humble offering."

"Certainly," replied the Guru. He asked one of them to open the lid. The moment the pot was opened, a foul smell filled the air. The honey had gone bad!

"B-b-b-but... how is that possible? How can honey go bad?" the pilgrims asked.

"That is because you refused to share the honey with one of my devoted followers. The Guru is never hungry for offerings. Whatever you give me is shared with my followers. By refusing Kattu Shah a taste of your honey, you have gone against my wishes – and that is to help the needy."

The pilgrims realised their mistake. They went back to Kattu Shah's humble cottage and made him a sumptuous meal to say sorry.

The pilgrims were shocked to see that the honey they had brought for the Guru had turned bad.

The Tenth Guru

Pir Bikhan Shah was a holy man who had many followers. One day, Pir Bikhan Shah and his **disciples** were getting ready for their evening prayers, when suddenly they saw a divine light in the east. Bikhan Shah immediately bowed in that direction. His disciples were surprised at their leader's strange behaviour.

"Oh, Holy One, why do you bow towards the east when we always bow towards the west during our prayers?" they asked.

Pir Bikhan Shah held out the two bowls of sweets and the little boy placed his hands on both of them.

"Today, I bowed towards the east because a special boy was born in a place that lies in the east. I must go and see this little boy, as he was sent by God to fight evil," the pir replied. So the pir set out to see the boy.

On his way, Bikhan Shah bought two bowls of sweets – one from a **Hindu** shop and one from a **Muslim** shop. He then went to the house where the child was and placed the bowls in front him. "Which bowl of sweets do you prefer?" he asked the boy.

The little boy placed his hands on both bowls at the same time as if to say that both were equally important to him. Pir Bikhan Shah looked at the child with wonder. "Today, I feel blessed that I have met such a great soul," he said smiling.

Bhikan Shah was not mistaken. The little boy was indeed destined for greatness. He was to become Guru Gobind Singh – the tenth Guru of the Sikhs.

▲ During the festivities, Sikhs show how traditional weapons were used.

Holla Mohalla

Holla Mohalla is an important Sikh festival. It is celebrated during the month of March and lasts for three days. Colourful parades, mock fights and horse-riding competitions form a major part of the celebrations. The festival was started by Guru Gobind Singh, who thought that mock battles would help his soldiers fight better.

The Khalsa

The Khalsa is a group of people who have pledged themselves to be true to Sikh teachings. The Khalsa has very strict rules. The most important of these is to wear the **Five Ks**: kesh (hair that is never cut), kanga (a wooden comb), kara (a steel bracelet), kacha (cotton underwear) and kirpan (a short sword).

▼ A **baptised** Sikh has to wear the five Ks at all times.

Guru Gobind Singh was only nine years old when he became the tenth Guru of the Sikhs, but he was determined to be a good leader. Soon he became one of the most popular of all the Sikh Gurus.

One day, at **Baisakhi**, an Indian harvest festival, Guru Gobind Singh asked his followers to gather at Anandpur Sahib in Punjab, India. Thousands of Sikhs gathered at the holy city, wondering why the Guru had invited them.

Guru Gobind Singh came out of his tent, drew his sword out and asked, "Who is ready to sacrifice himself?" The crowd stared in horror.

Suddenly, a voice rang out, "**Guruji**, my life is yours." It was Daya Ram, a devout Sikh. He accompanied the Guru into his tent.

A few minutes later, Guru Gobind Singh reappeared, blood dripping from his sword. "Who is next?" he asked, and another man followed him into the tent.

The Guru repeated this ritual three more times. He finally came out of the tent with the same five men. "You shall now be known as the Panj Pyaras, or the Five Beloved Ones. You shall be baptised with holy water and form the Khalsa," the Guru said amid cheers from the crowd.

Guru Gobind Singh baptised the five men with the holy water and blessed them.

The Battle of Chamkaur

Guru Gobind Singh lived at a time when the **Mughals** were forcing all **Hindus** to become **Muslims**. The Sikhs refused to change their religion. Instead, they decided to fight the Mughals to protect their faith. Guru Gobind Singh had to fight many battles against the Mughals. One battle was fought on the banks of the River Sirsa at Anandpur Sahib in Punjab, India.

During this battle, Guru Gobind Singh and his army of Sikhs crossed the river and reached a town called Chamkaur Sahib.

Sahibzada Ajit Singh fought bravely against the powerful Mughal army.

The Guru was accompanied by a small number of Sikhs, including his two older sons – **Sahibzada** Ajit Singh and Sahibzada Jujhar Singh. A few arrows, swords and spears were all they had left to help them fight the mighty Mughal army.

Guru Gobind Singh knew that the Mughals would come to Chamkaur Sahib looking for him, and they did. The Guru and his men immediately took up their positions around the fort and another fierce battle began.

The Sikhs soon ran out of arrows. "**Guruji**, what do we do now?" the followers asked their leader.

"Father, allow me to go out and fight the Mughals," the young Sahibzada Ajit Singh said. The Guru blessed his son and sent him out to take on the Mughals. The young man fought bravely. He killed many Mughal soldiers before being killed himself.

▲ The Gurdwara Garhi Sahib stands at the site of the Chamkaur Fort.

Supreme Sacrifice

The Battle of Chamkaur was one of the most important battles in the history of Sikhism. The **Gurdwara** Garhi Sahib marks the site of the fortress occupied by Guru Gobind Singh and his small army during the battle. It was built to remember the courage of all those who died during the battle Another place of worship, Gurdwara Qatalgarh, was built nearby on the battleground where the Guru's two sons and the rest of his army died.

▲ The Takht Sri Hazur Sahib at Nanded was built by the Sikh ruler Maharaja Ranjit Singh in 1839. It is one of the five holiest Sikh places in the world.

The Guru's Final Days

Guru Gobind Singh died on 7 October 1708 at Nanded in Maharashtra, India. It is said that an Afghan soldier entered the Guru's tent at night and stabbed him. Although the wound was treated, it did not heal well and the Guru died a few days later. A gurdwara now stands on the spot where he died.

Upon seeing his brother's heroic death, Sahibzada Jujhar Singh, who was only 15 years old, turned to his father. "Please allow me to take my brother's place in the battlefield," he begged. His father agreed. After a long fight, Sahibzada Jujhar Singh was also killed.

By the time it grew dark, only ten people, including Guru Gobind Singh, were left. The others begged the Guru to leave the fort.

"I will not flee the scene of a battle like a coward," he replied.

"But, Guruji, you are our strength. You must leave to build a new army and continue the fight against the Mughals," his followers insisted.

Guru Gobind Singh realised the truth in this and so agreed to leave during the night with three of his followers. They were in the forests of Macchiwara when Guru Gobind Singh received some desperately bad news.

His two other sons Sahibzada Fateh Singh and Sahibzada Zorawar Singh had been killed. Like their older brothers, the two boys had also died defending their faith.

"My fours sons sacrificed themselves so that my thousands of other sons can live peacefully. I will continue fighting for them," Guru Gobind Singh vowed.

The news of the martyrdom of the four Sahibzade made the Sikhs stronger and they continued fighting the Mughals until they won.

Sahibzada Jujhar Singh was blessed by his father before he went into battle.

Glossary

Baisakhi – a festival to celebrate the creation of the Khalsa or the Sikh religion. People who have joined the Khalsa wear the Five Ks. Baisakhi is also part of the harvest festival of Punjab, which takes place on 13 April every year.

baptism – ceremony in which a person is dipped in or sprinkled with holy water to symbolise that they are clean of sin and have become a member of the religion or church

communal – shared by the people of a community

Dev – a common Hindu name in India. The word means "god" in the Sanskrit language

disciple – follower or pupil of a saint or religious leader

Five Ks – the five symbols of the Sikh faith. They are called the Five Ks because each begins with the letter K in the Punjabi language.

gurdwara – place where Sikhs worship

Guru Granth Sahib – the Sikh holy book. It contains hymns and teachings written by the Gurus and other holy men.

Guruji – a respectful way of addressing a Guru

Hindu – person who follows the religion of Hinduism

langar – community kitchen attached to all gurdwaras. People from all religions and races are served free meals in a langar. *Langar* means "shared food".

Muslim – person who follows the religion of Islam

Mughal – **member of the group of** powerful Islamic people who ruled India and most surrounding areas from the early 16th to the mid-19th century

pir – Muslim saint or holy man

Punjabi – the language spoken in the Punjab region of India. *Punjab* means "lands of five rivers".

Sahibzada (plural: Sahibzade) – son of a teacher (Guru)

shabad – religious hymns or songs praising God, contained in the Sikh scriptures

Ten Gurus – the holy teachers and founders of Sikhism

Find out more

Websites

fateh.sikhnet.com/s/SikhStories
A collection of the 12 most popular Sikh stories for children.

www.sikhee.com/sikh-stories.html
An extensive compilation of stories from the faith. This website also contains a wealth of information on Sikh traditions.

www.sikhiwiki.org
An online encyclopaedia on Sikhism.

www.bbc.co.uk/religion/religions/sikhism
An excellent online resource that contains comprehensive information about the history, traditions, beliefs and festivals of Sikhism.

Books

The Milk and the Jasmine Flower and Other Stories by Anita Ganeri
Publisher: QED Publishing, 2007

My Sikh Faith by Kaval Singh
Publisher: Evans Brothers Ltd, 2006

My Sikh Year by Cath Senker
Publisher: Wayland, 2005

Sikh (Beliefs and Cultures) by Catherine Chambers
Publisher: Franklin Watts, 2003

Index